80% of the proceeds of this book will be donated to the NOHA Foundation.

Title: DVN-T City: Development for a New Time / Noha Saleeby
Summary: "In this book, Noha Saleeby puts forward a vision for sustainable growth. Readers are educated on the latest developments in sustainability, and then exposed to her project in the Democratic Republic of Congo where she is making her vision for a sustainable future into a reality."

The world is a global village whose "sustainable" development, today, is the responsibility of all of us. To reach this global scale, it is essential to start at the level closest to us.

Here is a book that will introduce us to one of the innovative projects, DVN-T City, which will be set up in the city of Kinshasa as a pilot project which will then be installed throughout the national territory, by spreading the project to the 145 territories, and then internationally thanks to the various partners of the foundation. This project is one of those accompanying the vision of the Head of State Felix A. TSHISEKEDI which aims at the development of the economy of our country.

The NOHA Foundation focuses on training, funding, and support for community self-development. It encourages creativity and innovation, it highlights audacious profiles capable of initiatives and sets up social facilities for the development of this community, it then creates a balanced life system.

With the sustainable development objectives thus set by world leaders, NOHA SALEEBY, in collaboration with the construction company INGENIO Consulting, is one of the development actors who have succeeded in setting up a project responding to the achievement of a number of Sustainable Development Goals (SDGs) as put forward by the UN. The DVN-T City project responds to several challenges facing the world and more particularly the DRC, namely poverty, environmental degradation, unemployment, to name but a few.

This book gives you the opportunity to see change from another angle by having as a guide the vision of Mrs. Noha S. who takes you into a world of awareness and decision. It is the aim that this book allows the popularization of the project of an ecological city which will be the image of the change so much wanted and awaited. This project is the result of years of reflection, research and training, the fruit of love from our company.

"Utopia for some, reality for others. I have chosen the certainty that my foundation will mark the 21st century through my unconditional involvement as a mother who has nothing but love to give and who accepts the mission of training, supporting and financing the community for its self-development. "

N. SALEEBY

The Foundress

Introduction

Several years of research and self-training in the fields of permaculture, agroforestry, eco-construction, alternative education, and many other subjects which are an integral part of the sectors essential to the development of Humanity have spawned the concept of a construction project that ensures sustainable development in our country and thus contributes to meeting global challenges.

From this, the DVN-T City construction project was born. The construction of a city corresponding to the model of sustainable development, focused on the growth in need of Man and nature in order to bring resolutions and bets on a circular economy system. An ecological city mainly composed of several areas including an agroforestry area, an agro-pastoral processing area, an area of 300 habitats, an educational area, a health area, and a cultural area. Urban development that wants to be in harmony with nature and our needs.

In this book, the redefinition of the term" need" put forward according to whether I want to perpetuate our values, which seem to be forgotten.

During this reading, I take you to the heart of a thought, that of a common well-being. It will seem illusory to you, but each of the following pages will open your mind to new perspectives for change.

I'm not talking about equality, because as Charles Gave said, *equality is taking from someone to give it to someone else, which requires doing it by force. It is roughly the source of all the crimes of the 20th century.* I'm talking about freedom, where we build a different future together while respecting everyone's freedom.

Take the time to stop, to breathe deeply to imagine a better world.

How do you see it?

....
....
....
....
....
....
....
....
....
....
....
....
....
....

Take a photo and send it to NOHAFONDATION@gmail.com

Now that your desires are laid down in black and white, what would you do to achieve them?

....
....

....
....

....
....

....
....

....
....

....
....

....
....

You are a fantastic person filled with qualities, gifts, skills, and an innate ability to put them at the service of those around you. Just turn on your internal switch to see yourself shine.

To illuminate a room, we do not put the lamp under the table but on the table, right? So go out and dare to fulfill your destiny.

This is exactly what I did after my realization of the state of humanity, I was devastated, everything seemed vain and meaningless.

I live in Angola, its capital city Luanda. This was on the list of the 3 most expensive cities in the world and yet more than 90% of the population lives below the poverty line. It is in this environment that day after day I was able to experience the social difficulties that the population braved to try to have a decent life.

Angola, well before the crisis, developed in ten years with oil as the only natural resource. We saw whole towns springing up, the latest brands of luxury cars driving at full speed and a marina where we could admire beautiful boats, which favored the social life of the Angolan population.

In 2016, the oil crisis arose. Brent (oil price) had fallen from 130 to its minimum of 30 (which did not cover the production cost of a barrel). Angola had not diversified its activities; its GDP was 90% dependent on the exploitation and export of oil and minerals. The installation of oil companies such as BP, Total, Chevron and so on, had caused rental prices to explode. A one-bedroom apartment in a miserable building could reach up to $5,000.00 per month and the owners demanded a full payment of one year's rent. For a single house this could go up to $30,000.00 per month with the same payment requirements. This situation had favored the emergence of a large middle class, but the crisis carried us away. It opened our eyes to the unsustainable and

"Magic" bubble in the country's economy. The country has been the victim of a major recession: a packet of sugar, 3 cans of peeled tomatoes, and various shortages are all that's left in the supermarkets. Not to mention the inflation due to the difficulty that companies have had in importing their merchandise.

1.   A question

I asked myself why, as a young entrepreneur, I found myself in a situation in which I have to sell my products in local currency at an absurd price, thus making accessibility reduced to an elite, thus ensuring the continuity of my activity which had become devoid of meaning? It was exactly during this period that I began to take an interest in the development of the country, to analyze what has been done in the past, the current state of the country, the existing resources and those which can be developed internally. The solutions were there before our eyes, we had everything, absolutely everything to self-develop the country, a rich and fertile land, an ambitious and hardworking youth, abandoned buildings, a lot of waste, a united people. What more do we need?

A structured design where everyone benefits. To drink, eat, have a roof over your head, education, health care, culture and work are no longer a utopia but become a reality for the population.

What do you think?

....
....

....
....

....
....

....
....

2.   Let's talk agriculture

I'll tell you the story of the $15,000 tomato.

Passing through the DRC, on a Sunday in May 2022, I was sitting
quietly in the living room at my grandmother's. Her caretaker asks me to
take her to the supermarket to buy tomatoes. In the vegetable
department, the display of prices was simply outrageous! We paid 10
US dollars for two tasteless tomatoes from Europe. I asked the lady
companion why this choice? Why not buy local food knowing they are

more nutritious. She replies: "Ah! you know for your grandmother, everything that comes from Europe is better. The majority of wealthy people in the country think that what comes from the West is better".

World leaders in the agricultural sector have succeeded in destroying European and American soils, making them dependent on chemicals that deplete the soil and in turn pollute groundwater. These leaders have not stopped in the West and continue their destruction on African soil.

The tomato contains between 300 and 400 seeds depending on the variety, each seed produces a plant which gives 10 to 15 tomatoes. Let's take the minimum 300 seeds multiplied by 10 tomatoes that are sold to the end customer in the case of this supermarket at $5.00 this gives us a turnover for the exploitation of a single tomato of $15,000.00.

Now you see the urgency to reclaim agriculture locally, to produce our seeds and to diversify the cultivation of products. We can no longer leave the management of our primary need to a group of capitalists who have already demonstrated the humanitarian disaster they have created by wanting to dominate the world, with decisions that are profitable to them and in no way for the good of mankind. These same people sell genetically modified seeds that are sterile for reproduction, sell fertilizers and all the chemicals necessary for abusive monoculture.

We absolutely have to put an end to this pattern that is killing us slowly. We must be aware of this because today it is the biggest financiers who are buying land around the world and I promise you that they are far from caring about the well-being of man. We have seen in the sugar and tobacco industries how, through cunning and cuts, they have tried to silence the specialists who denounce the wrongdoings of their industries. While 30% of the population suffers from obesity and while in so-called developing countries, or rather countries whose development is stifled, famine is growing due to these facts, we can notice that industrialists clearly show the importance of controlling what we eat.

3.   Can we do otherwise?

Of course, each country must resume agricultural development and produce its own seeds, called organic seeds.

Let me remind you that 1 century ago the agricultural industry did not exist. And you don't have to go to university to learn how to plant cabbage!

First, there is no healthy and ecological food without sustainable agriculture that respects biodiversity.

Agroforestry is the solution. This consists in associating trees, crops, and animals within the same plot, to transpose into agriculture, operating principles valid in a forest. In other words, a natural functioning system that has always existed before industrialization overshadowed it.

Benefits of Agroforestry

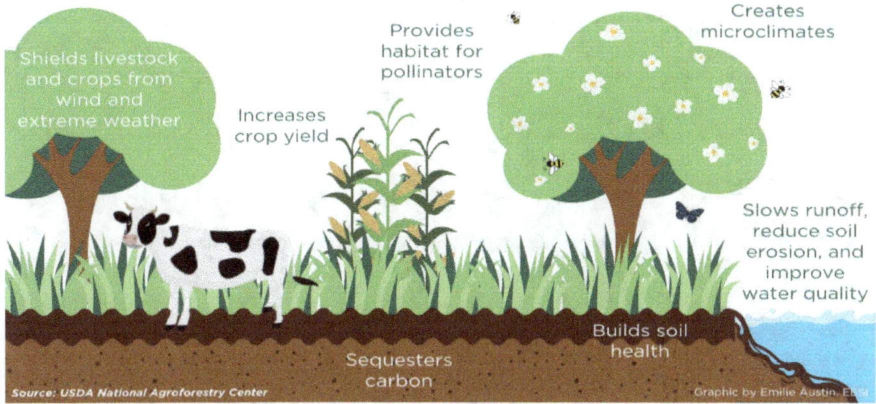

Source: EESI

The advantages of agroforestry are the increase in biodiversity, increase in organic matter nourishing the soil, the development of a microclimate at the scale of the plot, the increase in the yield of fields suitable for all types of crops, soils and climates. Agroforestry is accessible to everyone.

Agroforestry responds to the challenge of population growth by producing more food on smaller surfaces. It helps to ensure food self-sufficiency and at the same time regenerates the environment. It protects life rather than destroying it and fights global warming by sequestering carbon in the soil.

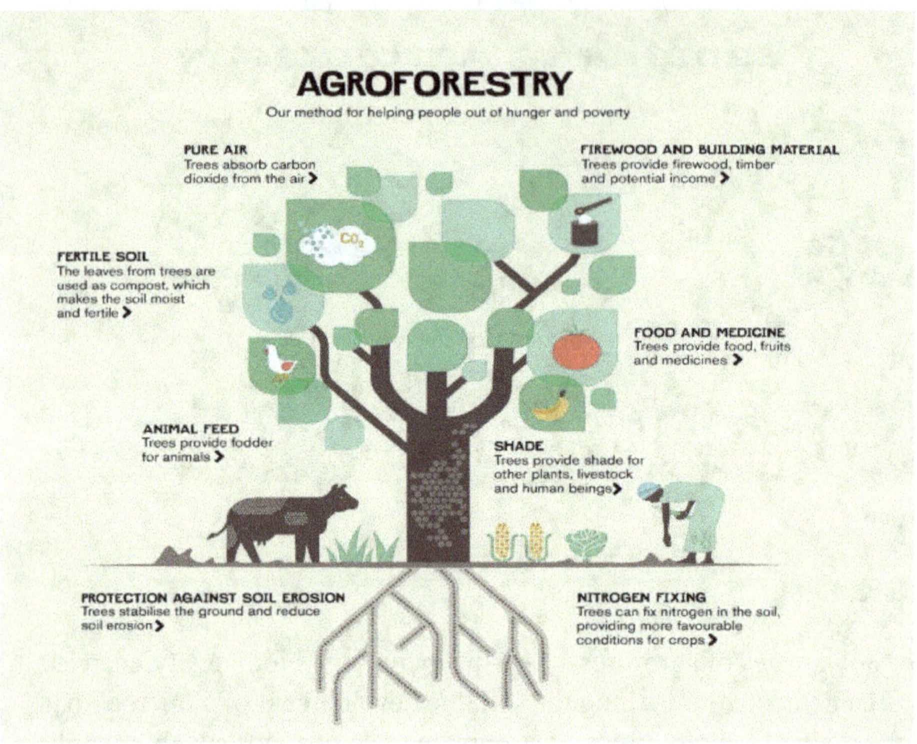

Source: <u>VI Agroforestry</u>

In the capitals of the world, we see the re-emergence of urban agriculture. On roofs, public spaces, terraces, community gardens and even in apartments, this activity that has always existed in cities or nearby for practical food supply reasons is the solution to meet the food shortage in urban areas. You should know that an area of one square meter can provide 20 kg of food per year. Urban agriculture creates a new economic activity starting from production, processing and distribution. It connects man to nature and restores social ties.

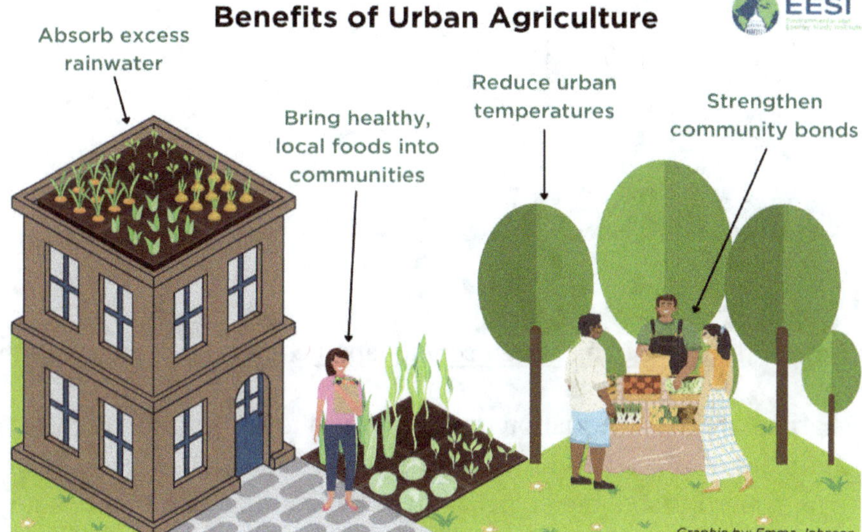

Source: <u>Environmental and Energy Study Institute</u>

The combination of aquaponics and urban agriculture is essential to diversify food sources and respond as shown in the diagram below to the organic production of urban agriculture.

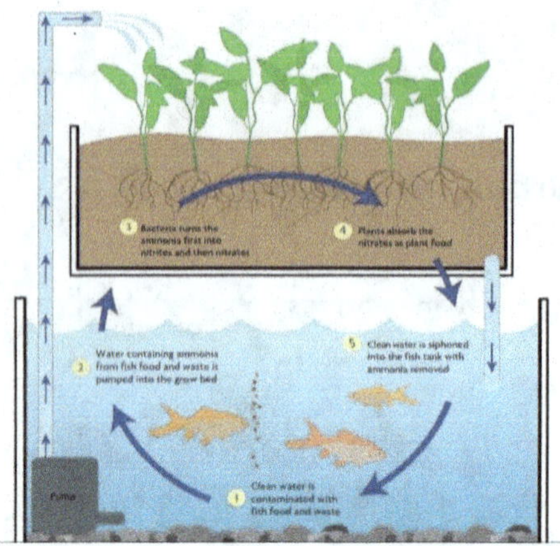

Source: https://mbgna.umich.edu/aquaponics-a-sustainable-solution/

Agricultural transformation must be linked to the space of the agricultural zone. This process makes it possible to have a series of companies in food, medicinal and cosmetic production in the same space, which would eliminate losses and increase job creation.

Examples:

-      The city of Detroit, which lost more than half of its population between the 1950s and 2000s, i.e., more than a million people, due to the economic and industrial crisis, has found its revival with the development of urban areas. Today, 1,500 farms and gardens are present in the city with 16,000 people involved.

-      Another urban farm like that of Toulouse was opened in Reims with the same principle having a more social objective. It is intended for people with low incomes or the homeless so that they can grow their vegetables in a public space, free of charge.

A roof for all!

Having a roof over your head is essential for every human being. There is no development without structure, without stability. Finland's social housing plan for the homeless is based on the principle of first providing housing and then supporting the person in their social reintegration.

It is said that we cannot understand a situation without having experienced it. Living in Angola, I had to readjust each time I faced a complicated economic situation due to the economic situation in the country.

There is no social assistance here. When you don't have a job, you easily find yourself in critical situations and very quickly become homeless. And it can happen anywhere and to anyone.

Solutions?

There are plenty of solutions here, I will mention 3:

-      Recovery by the state of abandoned real estate, renovating them by putting them on a crowdfunding platform.

-     Work with the designers of self-locking houses (assembled like Legos) made from recycled and ecological materials, thus offering the possibility to the inhabitants to build their own housing (participatory construction site). The State, by giving production spaces in each province and facilitating the installation of these companies, would see their territory urbanized without great difficulty.

-     Make available unoccupied state buildings for the development of temporary housing.

<u>Wind energy:</u>

Etymology "Aeolian" comes from the Greek Aiolos, meaning Aeolus, God of the winds in Greek mythology. The ancient form of the wind turbine is the windmill. In terms of purpose, a wind turbine is a system with rotating wings or blades to capture the kinetic energy of the wind and use it for purposes such as grinding grain or generating electricity. Wind energy is said to be renewable because it is 100% clean: it works thanks to natural and inexhaustible source winds.

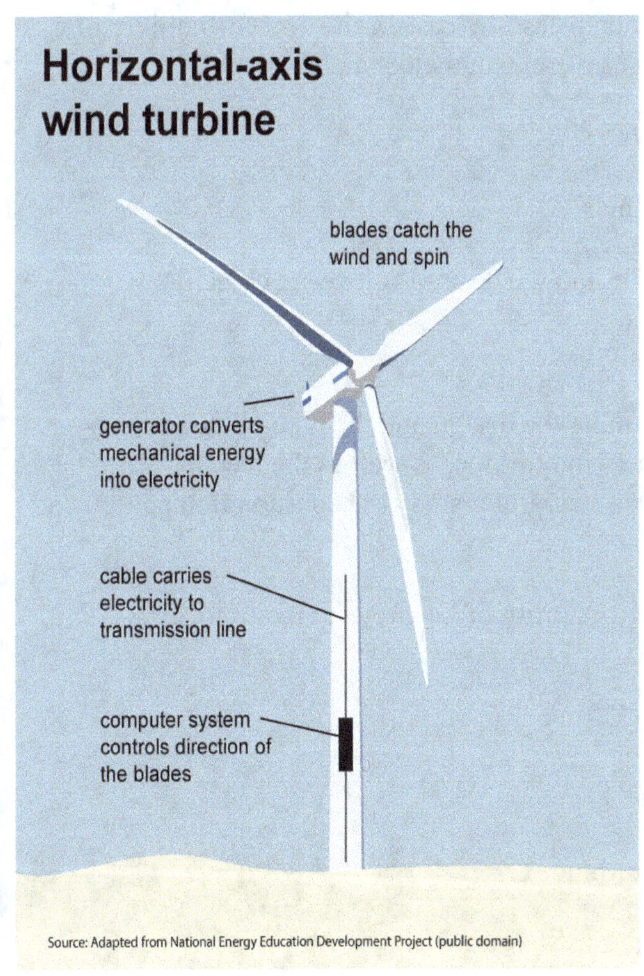

Source: Adapted from National Energy Education Development Project (public domain)

Source: https://www.eia.gov/energyexplained/wind/types-of-wind-turbines.php

The major drawback of this energy remains its difficulty in predicting it. Indeed, the winds are difficult to anticipate.

It needs a minimum amount of wind to start and stops working in case of winds above 90 km/h.

A feasibility and profitability analysis requires a thorough assessment that must be carried out on a case-by-case basis. The profitability of a wind project depends on several parameters including:

• the wind resource on the site

• the characteristics of the site

• the consumption profile and the desired autonomy objective

• the possible need for storage

These factors will determine the design and the type of the project, namely the power of the wind turbine, as well as the technology to be preferred. It is advisable to carefully study the consumption pattern and get help from a specialist.

The evaluation of the profitability of the project takes into consideration:

• the estimated producible

• the price of electricity

• the price of the wind turbine

• the financial aid granted

<u>Hydro-electric power</u>

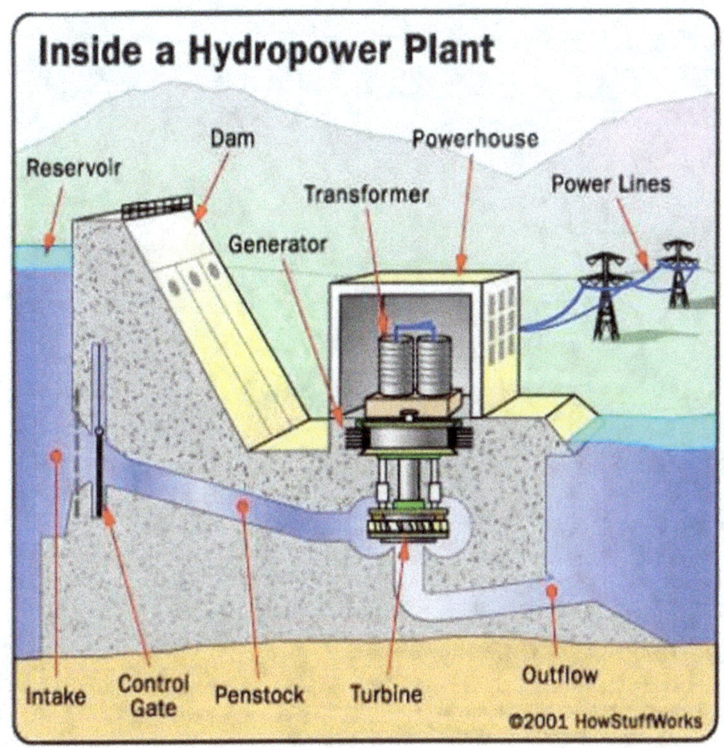

Source: https://smartwatermagazine.com/q-a/what-a-hydroelectric-power-plant-and-how-does-it-work

A hydraulic unit is made up of 3 parts:

- The dam that holds back the water
- The plant that produces the electricity
- Power lines that evacuate and transport electrical energy

It makes it possible to produce electricity in hydroelectric power stations, thanks to the power of water. This force depends either on the height of the waterfall (high or medium head power stations), or on the flow of rivers and rivers (run-of-river power stations).

Biomass

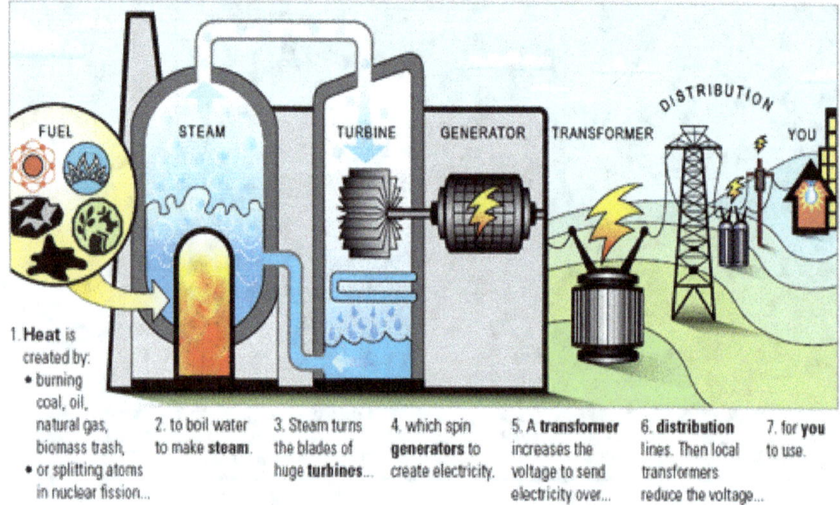

Source: https://my.xcelenergy.com/s/energy-portfolio/biomass

Biomass energy is a renewable energy source that depends on the cycle of living plant and animal matter.

Biomass energy is the oldest form of energy used by man since the discovery of fire in prehistoric times. This energy makes it possible to produce electricity thanks to the heat released by the combustion of these materials (wood, plants, agricultural waste, organic household waste) or biogas resulting from the fermentation of these materials, in biomass power plants.

Biomass by combustion

Waste is burned directly producing heat, electricity or both (cogeneration). This concerns wood, waste from wood processing industries and agricultural plant waste (straw, sugar cane, peanuts, coconuts, etc.).

The Dalkia Wastenergy (subsidiary of Dalkia, itself a subsidiary of EDF) urban waste incineration plant in Ivry-sur Seine (Val-de-Marne) treats the household waste of more than 5 million inhabitants (i.e., more than 690,000 tons per year).

In France, 10% of biomass electricity production comes from the combustion of biogas.

Biomass by anaerobic digestion

The waste is first transformed into a biogas, by fermentation using microorganisms (bacteria). The biogas is then burned. This biogas is close to natural gas and mainly composed of methane. This concerns household waste, animal manure and slurry, sludge from sewage treatment plants, paper, and cardboard, etc.

Geothermal

Geothermal energy brings together all the applications that make it possible to recover the heat contained in the subsoil or the underground water table and then transform it into energy.

Geothermal energy consists of exploiting underground heat to generate electricity or for heating. Unlike fossil fuels such as oil or natural gas, this technique uses a stock of inexhaustible and free energy. Indeed, the heat that comes from the center of the Earth is unlimited.

The different types of geothermal energy:

- _Very low energy_ (less than 30°C)

This process exploits the heat of the ground which is less than 100 meters deep and whose temperatures are less than 30°C. This technique is generally used for the heating and air conditioning of a home or to produce hot water.

- _Low energy_ (30 to 100°C)

This type of geothermal energy is based on the use of heat from aquifers at a temperature between 30 and 100°C. It is often used in various fields such as the air conditioning of agricultural greenhouses and the desalination of seawater. Cold countries also use it to prevent the accumulation of ice and snow.

- _High energy_ (over 100°C)

High-energy geothermal energy is intended to generate electricity for industrial uses. Its exploitation is done in specific regions of the globe such as sedimentary basins or volcanic regions. The steam is used to spin turbines for electricity generation.

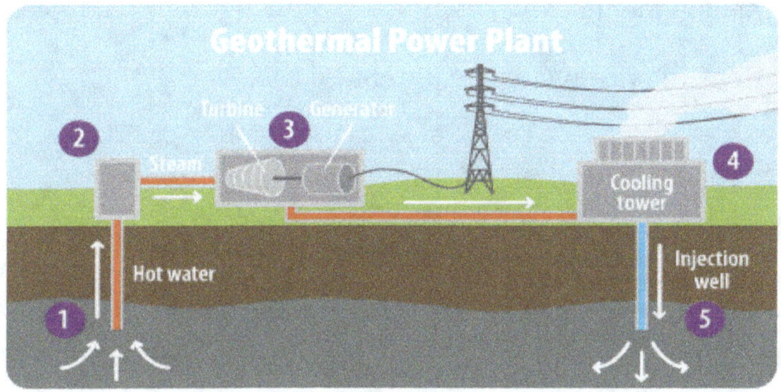

Source:
https://archive.epa.gov/climatechange/kids/solutions/technologies/geothermal.html

The energy mix to meet consumer demand.

Electricity producers must compose an "energy mix" from the various energy sources available on the market, because the electricity that powers your home is produced when you use it.

Choosing clean, local electricity costs the consumer a little more, in particular because of the costs associated with the construction of new installations. But it also encourages suppliers to invest in this sector in turn and thus strengthen the transition to electricity production composed mainly of renewable energies.

Water

<u>Wastewater management</u>

Here are the steps of wastewater treatment.

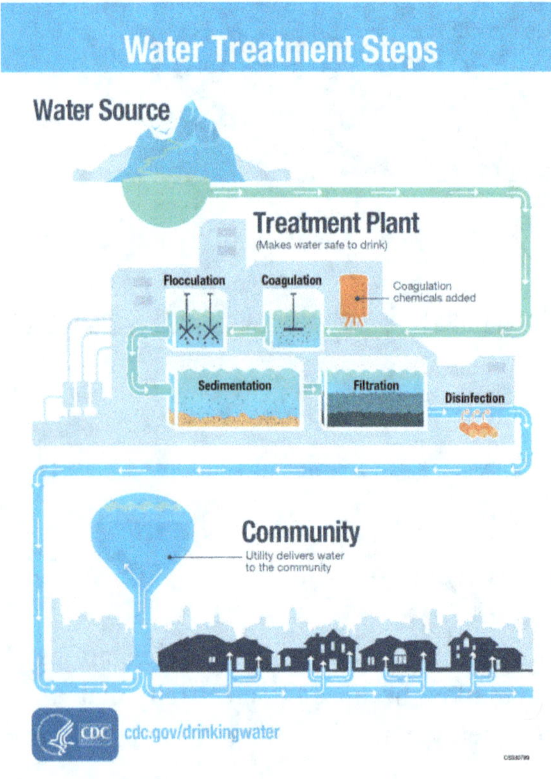

Source:
https://www.cdc.gov/healthywater/drinking/public/water_treatment.html

Phyto-purification uses bacteria in the root systems of plants to purify water.

In Phyto-purification, the plant Phragmites Australis (common reed) is most often used because it transforms organic matter and fixes heavy metals as well as products derived from detergents.

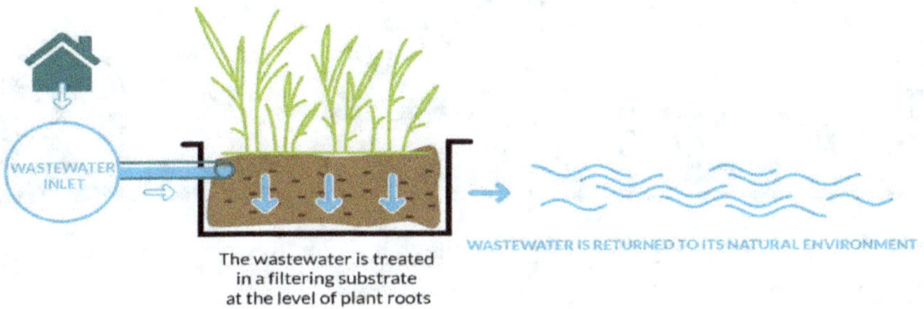

Source: https://www.aquatiris.fr/en/our-products/phytoflottantes/

Circuit recovering water from sinks, showers and washing machines to supply toilet flushes and the roof garden.

Home Graywater Recycling System

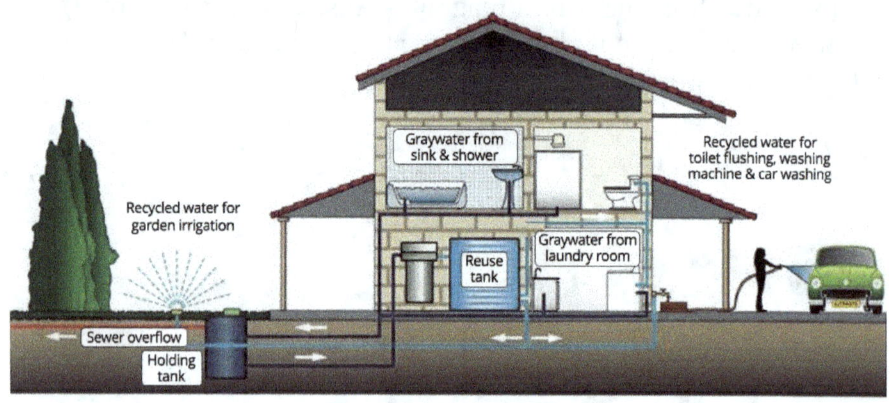

Source: https://www.alleghenyfront.org/allegheny-county-eyes-code-update-for-home-gray-water-systems/

Authorized uses

Gray water is wastewater that does not contain feces: domestic water from sinks, washbasins, showers, baths, dishwashers, washing machines.

According to the National Agency for Food, Environmental and Occupational Health Safety (ANSES), subject to the implementation of treatment and appropriate risk management measures, treated gray water can be suitable for the following domestic uses:

- Supply toilet flushes

- Water green spaces (excluding vegetable gardens and agricultural uses)

- Wash the exterior surfaces without generating aerosols (without using a high-pressure cleaner).

This recovery thus promotes a more closed water circuit within the building, making it possible to reduce the quantity of (drinking) water necessary and to reduce the flow evacuated towards the sanitation and purification infrastructures.

Rainwater harvesting

The rainwater that you collect must have only flowed over a roof that is not accessible (except to ensure its upkeep and maintenance). Water storage must be done in an above-ground or buried tank.

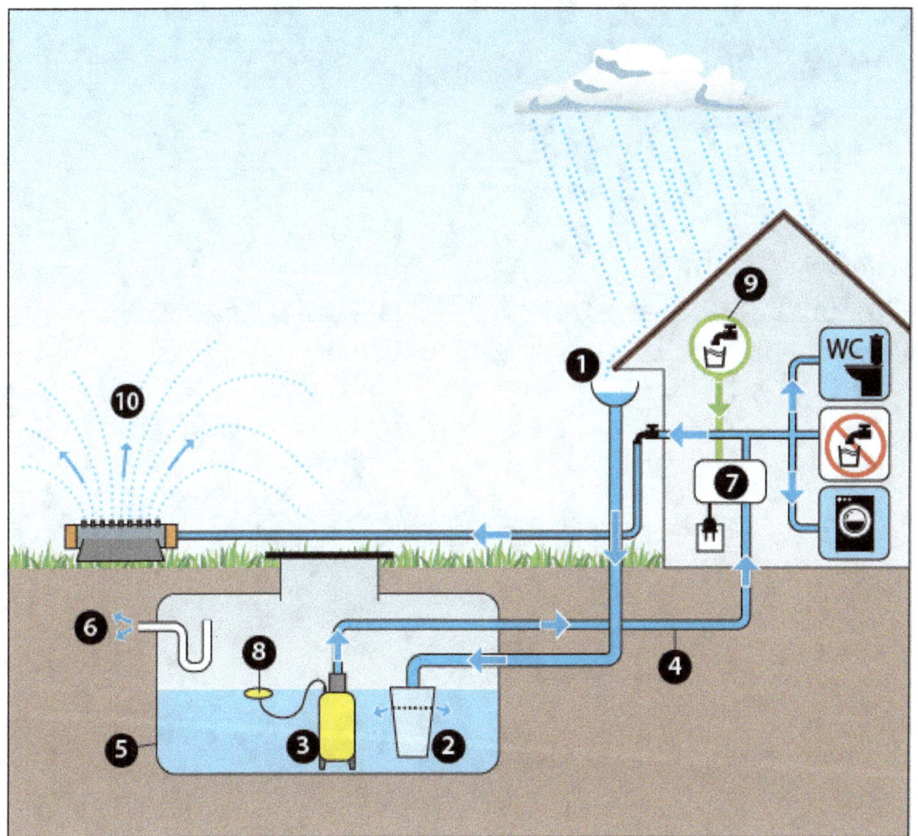

Short circuit treatment of waste

Our waste: a gold mine!

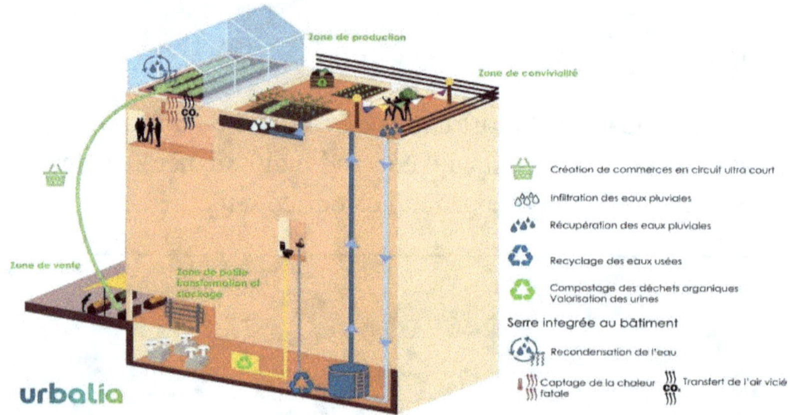

Source:
https://www.construction21.org/france/amp/articles/h/agric.ulture-utrbaine-en-ysymbolise-avec-le-blatiment.html

Education

My last 3 years of high school I spent in a small school; of a hundred students, after having changed school and city more than a dozen times, I finally had a break. School was an important refuge for me. I have always been attached to my studies, but this school gave me back a place in a "big family", helped me find a balance. We weren't mere numbers, but young girls and young boys surrounded by more attentive teachers because they didn't have the pressure of managing thirty students per class. We felt confident to help the youngest and be helped by our elders.

We all have the right to quality education, we just must restructure the national education organization, stop making "educational" factories, but design institutions on a human scale.

Conceptualize smaller neighborhood infrastructure that can accommodate 200 children including housing for teachers and a garden for agriculture; practical, simple, and inexpensive solutions that are easy to implement. Solutions that would serve as the basis for infrastructural development for viable and sustainable education. An infrastructure that would be autonomous once in place.

Adapt learning to the child, do you know the multiple intelligences?

1.   *Logical-mathematical intelligence:*
Develops abilities such as logic, analysis, observation, problem solving. Is in high demand in math and science classes.

2.   *Verbo-linguistic intelligence:*

This form highlights the mastery of the verb orally and/or in writing. It is also the intelligence of sounds. It allows you to master the language but also foreign languages. People with this intelligence have an above-average passion or talent for learning languages.

3.   *Visual-spatial intelligence:*

Is a component of cognitive intelligence. It mainly solicits sight and visual memory. This intelligence is solicited in courses such as geometry, geography, in artistic disciplines (photo, media, architecture, fashion, etc.). It is the ability to create images, to represent objects in space.

4.   *Intrapersonal Intelligence:*

It is the ability to know oneself, to reflect on oneself, to know how to listen to one's own feelings and needs.

5.   *Interpersonal Intelligence:*

It is the skill of being able to act and react appropriately with others in different contexts. This form of intelligence makes it possible to solve relational problems between individuals.

6.   *Body-kinesthetic Intelligence:*

It is the ability to control the movements of one's body to achieve a specific objective but also to express an idea or a feeling with it.

7.   *Musical-rhythmic Intelligence:*

It is the capacity to be able to think in rhythms and melodies, to hear and recognize, to memorize, to interpret and to create musical pieces.

8.   *Naturalist Intelligence:*
It is the ability to observe, appreciate, recognize, gather information on fauna, flora, and the mineral world.

Each child has potential, and it is possible to reach this potential without constraint:

In the school environment, many of the different forms of intelligence are often not called upon, whereas learning to recognize and use them allows the child to develop according to his interests and to discover himself in order to acquire the skills that she needs.

Today's school system does not prepare us for tomorrow's society. Most of our children find it difficult to integrate into the stagnant pedagogy; the world is changing but our education system is not.

Foster empowerment and free thinking:

According to LinkedIn, creativity and innovation will be key points in the recruitment of tomorrow. Firstly, because they cannot be copied by artificial intelligence and secondly, because the internet (zero marginal cost) has multiplied the possibilities in terms of innovation. But school does not prepare us at all for this. From year to year, children lose their freedom of mind and their ability to produce different visions of reality because the school penalizes what does not conform to books and lessons.

Work together:

The ability to initiate is increasingly in demand in large companies, while our school system does not prepare us for this. School projects should be more numerous and much more valued. This would have two benefits: first, as for an entrepreneur, there would be failures, successes, and therefore more complete learning. Second, it would develop group cohesion and promote mutual aid; which is not inculcated in the current system.

From the 19th century, Tolstoy, who is one of the most famous and read writers in the whole world, condemns the *interference of* the master on the student, that is to say his conscious influence. He refuses this " *forced influence of one person on another, with the aim of forming a man such as it will seem good to him* ". Thus, he goes so far as not to recognize "the *right to education*".

"Our *so-called science of the laws of good and evil and their action on a young generation is most often only an obstacle to the development of the new consciousness of our generation, a consciousness not yet elaborated, but which is being elaborated in the next generation: it is an obstacle and not an aid to education.* "

In recent years, new concepts of private schools, called alternative schools have emerged; the alternative school covers pedagogical currents that make the child an actor in his own learning. Also called active pedagogies, these alternative pedagogies , based on a benevolent approach, differ from traditional pedagogy insofar as they do not impose, as within the National Education, the authority of a teacher, a program preset, grades, penalties.

Examples:

-       Nature schools or Forest School: the development of the link with nature
-       Montessori schools: sensory education
-       Freinet schools: cooperation for learning
-       Steiner-Waldorf schools: awakening natural curiosity.
-       School at home or homeschooling: tailor-made schooling
-       Sudbury Alternative Schools or Democratic Schools: Experiential Learning
-       Schools of the 3rd type: self-directed learning
-       Schools with active pedagogy: the DNA of alternative pedagogy
-       Alternative, benevolent, and humane schools
-       The Reggio schools: the blossoming of creativity

The main objective is to allow children to act alone and think for themselves without going against their natural rhythm of development.

Man can no longer live away from his food source. While developing my analysis, I realized that we have divided everything into housing, work, education, health, and culture.

We must design on a human scale and restore the balance of our lives.

THE DVN-T CITY MODEL: A CONCEPT FOR SUSTAINABLE AND HUMANISTIC URBANIZATION

DVN-T CITY

I.

What is DVN-T CITY?

DVN-T CITY is a 40-hectare urban planning project oriented according to the principles of environmental preservation which integrates various housing modules, shops and services, tourist complexes, modern administrative and business buildings, numerous multifunctional spaces that include several educational complexes, hospitals, retirement homes, nurseries, training, and research centers.

Indeed, DVN-T CITY joins the principles of ecological urban planning, and that of the new city oriented on respect for the environment while developing activities with circular interests.

In addition, the city includes a policy to gradually reduce greenhouse gas (GHG) pollution within the city. Promote carpooling and focus on travel by means of eco-transport.

DVN-T CITY is a concept of sustainable development. This concept brings suitable solutions to the problems of life of our era.

As a result, it includes homes built with ecological, recycled, and recyclable materials; a security system; an internal trade and economic policy leading to regional tontines and also access for all to the alternative shopping Center. The large ecological park of DVN-T CITY; a cultural center for events and art workshop open to any artist; a large library and a large multidisciplinary training center; an orphanage with an adapted educational system, an industrial zone including a buffer zone to produce biomass, photovoltaic energy (photovoltaic power plant), wastewater and rainwater recovery zone as well as the treatment plant for drinking water. The key to sustainable development lies in the combination of technologies, organizational innovations, and lifestyle changes.

From the above, DVN-T CITY asserts itself as the bible of well-being and healthy living thanks to the various solutions it provides in its fields of activity.

II.

<u>ROJECT OBJECTIVES</u>

DVN-T City will meet the following Sustainable development goals.

DVN-T CITY Sustainable Development Goal 1 (SDG1): NO POVERTY

Sustainable Development Goal 8 (SDG8): DECENT WORK AND ECONOMIC GROWTH

Sustainable Development Goal 9 (SDG9): INDUSTRY, INNOVATION, AND INFRASTRUCTURE

DVN-T CITY, pilot project objectives:

-

ultivate notions of ecology

- Create local jobs
- Recycle waste in short and closed circuits
- Protect the local environment
- Integrate permaculture and food forests
- Reintegrate biodiversity
- Create a Community Interest Center

III.

<u>DVN-T City, Ecological City</u>

The creation of an ecological city is the solution to the demographic growth of cities, to relieve congestion in our capitals by offering spaces governed by the rules of sustainable development. Indeed, in the next twenty years, the urban population will represent nearly 80% of the world's population. Sustainable development is a major societal issue and the conditions under which its principles will have to be recognized and implemented challenge society in its various components.

Create an artificially modified ecosystem that has the qualities and characteristics of a natural ecosystem but offers more goods and services. It will bring necessary modifications to nature in order to grant it the means to find a balance for a common life of the species.

The project will therefore affect several compartments of the environment and therefore several types of ecosystems such as: the terrestrial, aquatic, and air-terrestrial ecosystem.

It should also be noted that the fence of the city will be made of trees. This will guarantee maximum air points and carbon sinks. The buildings will be made of ecological fired bricks and other recycled, recyclable, and ecological materials. The city will use green energy from photovoltaics and biomass (thanks to the collection of dry toilet materials).

III. 2. *DVN-T CITY, Economic city*

DVN-T CITY offers opportunities for young entrepreneurs to exhibit their products in the alternative shopping center at low rents; to obtain a low-rent office also in the administrative building; the city also offers young entrepreneurs the possibility of paying for one of the 300 social houses.

Another economic advantage of the city is that it remains open to leave agricultural space and industrial buildings to agripreneurs and other entrepreneurs with industrial vocations.

From the above, the city will proceed with a regional tontine policy which will be controlled by the central administrative office in order to allow the empowerment of young entrepreneurs in the region. The social houses will either be rented, sold, or loaned.

III. 3. *DVN-T CITY, a technological city*

DVN-T CITY will be the first city in the Congo to set up: (1) a photovoltaic power plant; (2) the use of efficient dry toilets; (3) power plant with biomass; (4) digitized remote control police station; (5) station for recycling and treating rainwater and wastewater for consumption.

III.4. *DVN-T CITY, a tourist town*

The city will be a good tourist setting thanks to its local architecture and the activities that will be planned there (festivals, concerts, cinema, etc.).

DVN-T CITY will contain an ecological park, a cultural center, an art workshop, an exhibition hall, a large restaurant, lodges, a spa, as well as a sports center.

III.5. _DVN-T CITY, a scientific city_

The DUNAMYS multidisciplinary training center was designed to make training accessible to people wishing to find a job that lives up to their dreams. The training center offers 26 quality training courses with the possibility of internships and employment in the city thanks to the number of companies and activities present.

DVN-T CITY will also include a school to ensure the schooling of the children of the city and the children living in the region where the city will be built. Research centers and libraries will also be included in this large educational building.

III.6. _DVN-T CITY, cultural city_

The large cultural center of DVN-T will provide an ideal setting for young artists to showcase their talents. The city will give to future artists its art studio, its showroom and its dance hall.

DVN-T CITY sees itself as the first city offering cultural activities that defy all competition. Shows, the festival, and other events will also be organized.

IV.
ONES AND SUBDIVISIONS

The city is subdivided into 4 blocks of 10 hectares each. Block 1 goes from the entrance of the city to the park; the second block is reserved only for dwellings; the third block is that comprising the educational, sanitary, hotel and sports buildings.

Ultimately, the fourth zone will include an industrial part and a buffer part. The city is also broken up into zones. These areas are divided according to activities and centers of interest to facilitate the interconnection of the city in order to make it vibrate.

DVN-T CITY will include a commercial zone, a tourist zone, a residential zone, a sports zone, an educational zone, an industrial zone, a health zone, and an agricultural zone.

The commercial area will include a large alternative shopping center which will house hair salons, clothing houses, banks, beauty salons, fresh meat from the city's slaughterhouse and local productions. It should also be noted that the terrace will have storage and cultivation space.

The administrative zone is an area comprising rental offices at low rents for businesses and the city management office.

The tourist area encompasses the large DVN-T City Park as well as restaurants (in the second block) and lodges (in the third block). This area is designed to create meeting points during major events in the city.

The cultural zone includes the cultural center as well as the art workshop which will allow the organization of artistic residences. This part of the city will boost the attendance of people within DVN-T CITY and will appear as one of the added values.

The residential area includes 300 dwellings. As pointed out in the previous paragraphs, the houses will either be sold or rented at prices accessible to the population. And for the employees of the city, their houses will be sold by fixed-term contract. The education zone will include the Institution la Colombe, a school, a training center, a library, a crèche, and a student home. This part of the city will open its doors to anyone wishing to learn with an adapted educational system.

The health zone will include the DVN-T Center hospital as well as the retirement home. Access to health will take precedence over any pecuniary desire.

The sports area will include the large sports center which contains a football, volleyball, basketball, and tennis court.

The industrial zone at the end of the concession will include large industrial buildings intended for the processing of agricultural products and products from the town's slaughterhouse; but also, some buildings will serve as warehouses and other uses.

The buffer zone will be chosen after a topographic study of the land to delimit the catchment area and the outlet. This area is our wastewater and rainwater collection point, there will be a drinking water treatment plant, a biomass power plant and a photovoltaic power plant.

The plan in hand, I now had to materialize it, but how?

In March 2020, I was going to Belgium to give birth. At the beginning of April, all the borders are closing. My return to Angola no longer had a date. I decided to open a company to start working on the project. The idea was to create a bridge between Europe and Africa for the development of ecological agriculture through a platform where developing projects would be exposed. The goal was to expose DVN-T City. They rejected the request to open the company. Not understanding the reasons, I made an appointment with an international legal firm. The Lawyer listened carefully to the project, I explained to him that I did not know the right approach to follow for the opening of the company, that I came to seek their expertise.

Taking a deep breath, he explained to me that my project is ambitious and that I had to be ready for people to attack me since I was directly attacking the agri-food industries, he added "we will be delighted to accompany you in this great adventure". After two hours of meetings, I came out of this interview totally determined to make it happen.

Portugal, then Spain to do a market study and complete my business plan were important destinations. I went there and visited in each of the countries, two agricultural villages and I was thus able to train myself on their management system and realize the crisis they were going through: there were several plots for sale everywhere I went. M explained that the production is owned by a large group that cuts prices, meaning the village is forced to stop their activity.

<u>THEY SUCCEEDED, WHY NOT US</u>

1.   *THE CUBAN MODEL*

In the 90s, Cuba experienced a terrible economic crisis called *the special period,* following the disappearance of the Berlin Wall, the dismemberment of Comecon (Organization *for Economic Mutual Aid between Eastern Bloc Countries, created in 1949 and dissolved with the end of the Soviet Union in 1991)* and disintegration of the USSR, not to mention the consequences of the financial blockade imposed by the United States. The result: crowded buses with passengers hanging from the doors to go to work, thousands of cars parked for months due to a lack of fuel, endless queues to obtain subsidized food at exorbitant prices, ...

As is often the case, the best solutions are born in misery.

The Cuban state has distributed tens of thousands of bicycles to work centers to be distributed to employees.

The breeding of chicken and pigs multiplied in the apartments, in the heart of the city, to meet the food needs of the family.

For months, homes were without electricity for much of the day.

This almost permanent break allowed families to meet after work on the corner of the street, on the roofs to tell stories, make jokes, and simply live together.

Key sectors such as education and health have continued to be ensured by the State's effort.

Urban agriculture, this reorientation of urban space and this new face given to agriculture was necessary to get the island out of famine. No longer having access to pesticides, chemical fertilizers… They had to develop agricultural techniques such as Permaculture and develop biological fertilizers.

A crisis that should have been fatal allowed a population to find alternatives to the codes of capitalism.

2.

THE AMISH

The AMISH, some of them seek remote corners so that the world does not stain their principles of belief, but that is not the question. They gather in a few families and with very little means, set up accommodation in 2 weeks and begin their plantation to consume and sell their production in the neighboring markets. So, what do they have more than us? Why has hunger become such a complicated story to settle? Why are we not able to build our own habitats? I ask it naively; we know the reasons well… But when are we going to accept them? It's a standoff that must be faced, the time of the ostrich is over.

3.

THE SINGAPOREAN MODEL

Singapore, devoid of natural resources, has today become one of the most prosperous economies in the world. Like Tokyo and Shanghai, it is one of the most advanced Smart Cities.

The keys to Singapore's success are Urban Planning and Mobility.

Everywhere in the world we are witnessing a change in the relationship to the car and more generally to private property, which applies a new relationship to services for the inhabitants. This transformation is global and changes everything!

Singapore, 700 km^2, which explains the need to develop and welcome all ideas helping to reduce the use of personal cars, such as buses and autonomous cars.

It is above all through public power, and the control it exercises over the land to which we owe the success of mobility in Singapore.

Singapore is one of the strongest cities in the world regarding Transit Oriented Development, TOD. Even if there is a free lease system, the land still belongs to the government.

The fact that it controls the ground gives it the ability to design and implement mixed-use projects around metro stations. These urban projects therefore mix habitats and employment areas.

Singapore, after creating efficient transport to bring people closer to their jobs, has created mixed areas: housing, jobs, leisure, shopping areas, schools. Then appeared new cities that connected to Singapore following the same urban concept.

Singapore has managed to include 20% green space (park, garden, etc.)

Singapore does not depend on private investors. And that is Singapore's great strength. The government has 100% control of the ratio between employment, the number of inhabitants and the companies that set up there. Thanks to the mastered planning tools it implements this truly is a Smart City.

Three totally different examples that could inspire us, not politically or religiously, but for their ability to find alternatives despite the realities not conducive to developments.

FEASIBILITY: CASE OF THE DRC

Sounds a bit complicated to set this up, doesn't it?

In any case, the first thing you will be confronted with, as in any ambitious and revolutionary project, is the criticism you will receive in your face! Good constructive criticism rarely, mostly discouraging and sometimes even insulting.

For me, here are a few:

"Where do you get your crazy ideas, you've gone mad, you should go get treatment"   Perpetrators: poorly educated family members.

"You don't think that other people have tried, and you really believe that you are going to succeed"   Author: an acquaintance with no ambition, vision, life project.

"You should focus on a small project, open a restaurant, keep calm, this kind of project will bring you a lot of trouble"   Author: a well-intentioned person.

"The project is very interesting, and you will disturb a lot of people. You realize that with this type of development the industrialists will not leave you in peace. You really need to protect yourself. We are ready to follow you"   Author: Group of lawyers from a Parisian firm.

"What do I win?"   Authors: a lot of people

What you must do is above all detach yourself from criticism, for those who are constructive, take the time to analyze them, it can only enrich your work. The rest does not concern you!

When you have the conviction that what you are doing will bring solutions, however small, to your family, to the people around you and even to the nations, don't let anyone pull you down. Hold on to your vision and have faith!

SO, HOW DO WE SET UP DVN-T CITY?

Take the Democratic Republic of Congo which has launched a development plan for the 145 territories, there you are saying to yourself "it must not be going well!" I assure you I have long studied the different possibilities and they are viable.

First, we must concentrate on carrying out a pilot project, the establishment of DVN-T CITY on 40 hectares made available by the State because this project must be semi-state within the framework of a public-private partnership (PPP) since it is designed for the development of the country.

The pilot project will serve as a training center. It should make it possible to set up teams which will themselves be divided to go to the territories, form local teams for the construction of the city. DVN-T CITY was designed to be built in 6 months with a budget of $50,000,000.00.

With the INGENIO team, a group of building engineers, architects, environmental experts, green energy experts, etc., whose founder Merdi Kashamankoy, adapted the construction project on Congolese territory.

A project of this magnitude requires the participation of different actors of Congolese society.

- Universities will be more than happy to work on a project where they can put their knowledge into practice;

- The construction companies to show their know-how, by proposing to them to build a model house at their own expense in return they would then be guaranteed a contract for the construction of several houses on the territories. They will have the obligation to form 3 teams to build one of their houses;

- General Kasongo who trains the kulunas (idle youth addicted to violence) for 1 year in the camp in Katanga in trades such as carpenter, builder, farmer… would enter this program and with a real social reintegration plan;

- Banks with a financing plan;

- NGOs and Foundations for social parties, hospitals, orphanages, schools, etc.

- Volunteers from here and elsewhere; by having a sustainable development project with a clear vision, an action plan and good communication, people will come by themselves;

- Artists for the cultural area; in Central Park, the lungs of New York, the park benches are named after donors who fund construction and maintenance. An honorable way to perpetuate its history;

-    Entrepreneurs like:

✓   RECOPLAST which transforms the plastic from our garbage cans (which invade the city, rivers, etc.) into building materials and furniture;

✓   KEMCO Innovation Sarl, a company that manufactures interlocking building blocks from all types of plastic waste;

✓   A young entrepreneur who found a process to make bags supporting up to 50 kg from banana leaves;

✓   JAMBO, our local fruit juice producer who travels the country with seeds to ensure the raw material and promotes local producers;

✓   Initiate a platform bringing together more than 500 entrepreneurs active in the Democratic Republic of Congo; Community of Investors, mainly from the diaspora, living in the 4 corners of the world with a single desire, that of wanting to come and invest in the country;

✓   Sultani Makutano which is a pan-African Congolese business network that organizes forums bringing together economic decision-makers to discuss the appropriation of the Congolese economy by locals and how to create national champions;

-    Investors who will not hesitate to participate in the project. By offering them solutions to secure their investments such as:

✓   Set up crowdfunding platforms;

✓   A digital management system to which they will have access.

CONTRIBUTION AND ROLE OF THE STATE IN THE IMPLEMENTATION OF DVN-T CITY

As part of the public-private partnership, the State's contribution will consist of:

- Provision of land to be used for the construction of DVN-T CITY housing estates;

- Finance the establishment of a study office specifically for the development of DVN-T CITY in the 145 territories as a basis for the urbanization of the territory;

- Finance the establishment of a business management office equipped with a management and investor search platform. Companies will put their accounts there… for the transparency of investors and the state ensures the smooth running of activities TRANSPARENCY = TRUST;

- Exemption of companies in the agro-business and recycling sector that settle in DVN-T CITY for a period of up to 5 years;

- Fiduciary and administrative support, business facilitation and integration of expatriates;

-	Support for the transport of equipment and teams.

THE DESIGN OFFICE

The design office will:

-	Produce feasibility studies that guide and justify the structural, strategic and technical choices of the spaces where DVN-T City will be established in the 145 territories;
-	Produce local urban plans: set the rules for development and land use;
-	The study office will have a central office in Kinshasa as well as cells in each territory.

Objective:

Perpetuate the model of eco-responsible urban development to avoid the development of anarchic urbanization.

<u>THE BUSINESS MANAGEMENT OFFICE</u>

The DVN-T City will have an economic zone which will aim to offer products and services to the inhabitants of the said city. DVN-T City aspires to offer an ecosystem that will allow local and foreign investors to invest in companies operating in the economic zone. To create trust with investors, DVN-T City intends to set up a transparent management office for these companies in order to allow said investors to have direct access to information related to the development of companies before and during their investments. The management office also supports the companies operating in the economic zone from a management point of view in order to ensure the efficient use of the resources invested by the partners of DVN-T City in these companies.

<u>COMMUNICATION STRATEGY</u>

The construction of the DVN-T City pilot project will be broadcast in the form of a reality show in order to show the world that it is possible to build eco-responsible cities or towns with the means of the country in a fast, innovative, inclusive, and inexpensive way.

The goal is also to encourage local, national, and international partners to mobilize resources and duplicate the project on a large scale, whether in other parts of the DRC or elsewhere.

This reality show will be produced by OMEGA PROD which is an audiovisual production company based in the DRC.

<u>WHY DVN-T CITY DRC?</u>

The demographic boom, economic and ecological issues are forcing the nation to rethink its urban planning.

Basically, Kinshasa is a city that was built for barely 10,000 inhabitants in 1910. Today it has more than 17 million inhabitants. becoming one of the largest agglomerations in the world, 3rd in Africa after Cairo and Lagos and the 1st French-speaking agglomeration. However, urban growth has not kept pace with population growth: number of housings, schools, hospitals per inhabitant, etc.

DVN-T City is a project that fits into the vision of the Head of State, Felix Antoine Tshisekedi who wants to attract foreign investors to the Democratic Republic of Congo, but also the return of the Congolese and African Diaspora to the DRC.

But for such a return to be possible and at the same time to attract these foreign investors, it is necessary to set up a whole favorable ecosystem which allows them to operate under the right conditions. This ranges from quality and inexpensive housing space to a local connection network with local operators and international investors through the so-called economic zone.

DVN-T CITY is also:

Facilitating rapid and less costly eco-responsible urbanization of the 145 territories, allowing, among other things, to relieve congestion in the capital and avoid massive rural exodus.

The project also creates an excellent living environment for the rural population integrating a system of organic and local farming within the city itself.

The project also brings producers closer to consumers through a short-circuit consumption system.

DVN-T CITY is a project with an economic impact through the creation of employment by hiring teams who will be trained for the construction of DVN-T cities in the 145 territories. But also, through the promotion of local entrepreneurship and the attraction of international investors in the economic zone.

DVN-T City is also a new face of the DRC to sell a positive image of the country which will boost the attractiveness in terms of investment and tourism.

DVN-T CITY is the materialization of a development towards new times. It takes the elements of our lives to harmonize with nature/earth and the nature of man. The objective is to put people back at the center of activities and humanize the world in which we are short-lived. We will see together the existing solutions brought up to date and other solutions adapted from different cultures.

We have the grace to be able to analyze the examples of urbanization that did not work:

- HLMs in France;
- New cities in Angola like Kilamba kiaxi, Zango;
- Abortion of the ecological urbanization project on a Chinese island designed for 500,000 inhabitants.

The failure of these urban planning projects mentioned above is due to the lack of integration of commercial, administrative and economic spaces, thus becoming landlocked cities.

Social housing is inseparable from the economic, political and human evolution of a country. In France, between 1875 and 1914, the urban population increased from 12 to 18 million, while the total population remained practically stable. In urban areas, overcrowding becomes the rule. In 1906, 62% of people living in towns with more than 5,000 inhabitants lived at 2 or more per room. Numerous surveys report the miserable living conditions of the workers, with significant spread of epidemics, in particular tuberculosis, which alone has caused several thousand deaths per year. Tell me, isn't that what we're going through now? Malaria and typhoid kill how many people a year?

Far too many forums, conferences, meetings of words and words, agreements where millions are released and then … nothing! The system is failing and benefits a small number of people in power, filling their pockets shamelessly with the result of poor people who see social inequality widening more and more.

Buildings are growing in the city of Kinshasa, rental price from $2,000.00 to $8,000.00 monthly rent. But who can afford it in a country where 90% of the population lives below the poverty line?

Is there an urbanization plan for our capital including decent social housing solutions? Neighborhood centers to help the poor? What about our orphans? Integrating urban agriculture zones, allowing to provide a basic basket to families, is it so difficult? Sanitation, there are so many solutions that citizens try as best they can to set up but are confronted with the abuse of the system and its lack of political will and organization.

Mobility? Is it so complicated to install trams, buses, minibuses, and a centralized and organized network?

Nothing is hard, everything is possible but apparently this total and anarchic confusion suits many!

REBIRTH OF KINSHASA

The components of a sector form a district, a homogeneous zone, by their resemblance and by their proximity.

District 1000 inhabitants:

-       A neighborhood center is headed by a neighborhood leader. The latter is the interlocutor of his municipality and a key player in the local development process;
-       Modern and digitized police station;
-       Construction of 500 dwellings: 70% of houses financed with a participatory financing system and 30% of social houses financed by the State or investors specialized in this sector;
-       Family planning: Popular education, civility, sex education, contraception, fight against violence. The actors: gynecologist, general practitioner, psychologist lending time on a voluntary basis (rotation system) can be supported by an NGO;
-       A neighborhood orphanage:

✓   Establishment that can accommodate 40 children;
✓   Set up alternating custody of volunteers, educators and neighborhood mothers;
✓   Paid extracurricular activity open to all, which would stimulate the children and meet the needs of the establishment;
✓   Set up a sponsorship system;
✓   Create a vegetable garden, beekeeping, poultry farming, fish farming in quantities studied for the nutrition of children and use this educational space to train children;
✓   Artistic courses where the objects will be sold on the establishment's website would make it possible to set up a bank account

for each of the children so that when they are old enough to take flight they will have a job and capital to start their life off;

✓ Crèche, school: draw inspiration from alternative educational systems, such as WALDORF 100, MONTESSORI, FREINET, CALVERT, and Finnish schools which are recognized for their very high performance in their education system. These schools are based on creative freedom and the development of children's autonomy from an early age;

✓ Installation of a commercial zone giving access to premises at low rental prices for entrepreneurs;

✓ House of Culture to leave an open space for the creation of artists from the district;

✓ Creation of a neighborhood bank for the tontine and its management;

✓ Green space park, participatory urban agriculture and medicinal plant garden;

✓ Recycling center: centralize waste;

✓ Rainwater recovery system and wastewater recovery/treatment;

✓ Biogas production plant with our waste/toilets.

Today the Lebanese crisis leads honest people to rob their bank to recover the money from their account, no more and no less. The inflation of the Lebanese pound is 80%. The country is ruined. Just to name one of the latest examples of the "humanitarian" crisis and we have countless of them...

Small changes can change everything!

Here is a model and some pictures of what DVN-T City will look like.

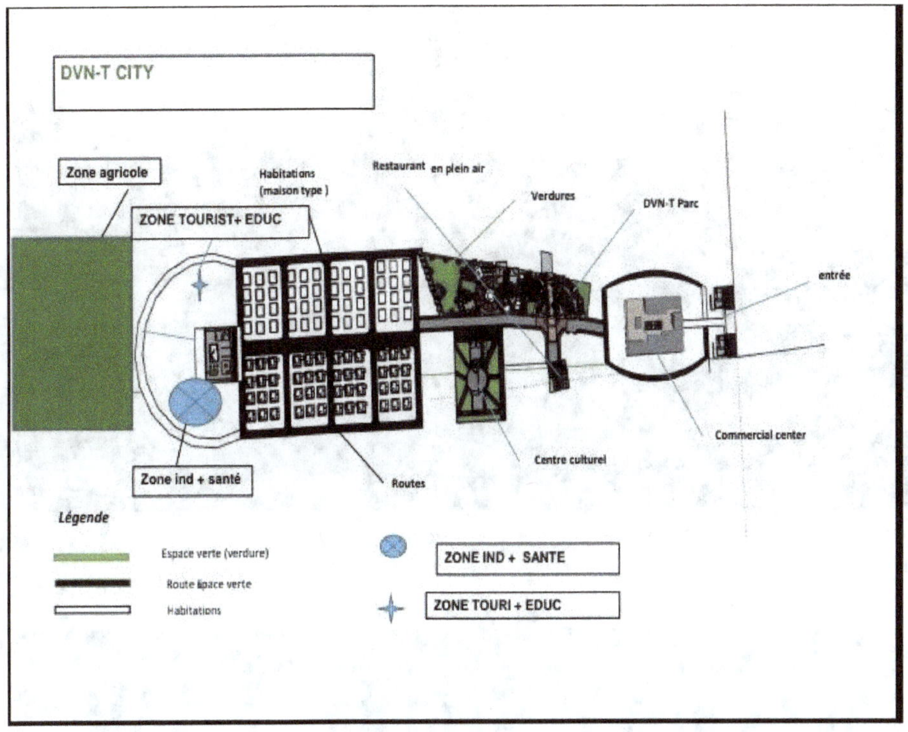

DIVINITY HOUSE

THE NOHA FOUNDATION: VISION, MISSION AND PROJECTS

I. <u>OUR VISION</u>

Seeing beyond the challenges and obstacles present in our communities is the ideal way to achieve our goal. The NOHA foundation aims for a community developed on all axes. Based on this, it aims more specifically:

✓ A community with sufficient knowledge to contribute to the various local development projects;

✓ A full development of local entrepreneurs who will be financed by the foundation and

✓ Follow-up and support to maintain the momentum towards new horizons.

II. <u>OUR MISSION</u>

The main mission of NOHA FOUNDATION is to provide support in projects of common utility to promote culture and creation, to encourage research and education, and to act for a sustainable environment.

III. <u>OUR PROJECTS</u>

The DVN-T CITY project is currently the main project of the foundation. This project will allow us to achieve our vision and accomplish our mission in the local community and throughout the national territory with the support of the Congolese State to promote the Public-Private sector.